CW00542625

by Ann Lindsay Mitchell

LangSyne
PUBLISHING
WRITING *to* REMEMBER

Lang**Syne**

PUBLISHING

WRITING *to* REMEMBER

79 Main Street, Newtongrange,
Midlothian EH22 4NA
Tel: 0131 344 0414   Fax: 0845 075 6085
E-mail: info@lang-syne.co.uk
www.langsyneshop.co.uk

Design by Dorothy Meikle
Printed by Printwell Ltd
© Lang Syne Publishers Ltd 2022

ISBN 978-1-85217-042-4

Farquharson

SEPT NAMES INCLUDE:

Barrie
Bowman
Brebner
Christie
Coutts
Findlay
Findlayson
Finlay
Finlayson
Greusach
Hardie
Hardy
Kerracher

Maccaig
MacCartney
Macearacher
Macfarquhar
Machardie
MacHardy
Mackerachar
Mackerracher
Mackindlay
Mackinlay
Reoch
Riach
Tawse

Farquharson

MOTTO:
By Fidelity and Fortitude.

CREST:
A demi lion Gules holding
in his dexter paw a sword proper.

TERRITORY:
Upper Deeside in Aberdeenshire.

Chapter one:

The origins of the clan system

by Rennie McOwan

The original Scottish clans of the Highlands and the great families of the Lowlands and Borders were gatherings of families, relatives, allies and neighbours for mutual protection against rivals or invaders.

Scotland experienced invasion from the Vikings, the Romans and English armies from the south. The Norman invasion of what is now England also had an influence on land-holding in Scotland. Some of these invaders stayed on and in time became 'Scottish'.

The word clan derives from the Gaelic language term 'clann', meaning children, and it was first used many centuries ago as communities were formed around tribal lands in glens and mountain fastnesses.

The format of clans changed over the centuries, but at its best the chief and his family held the land on behalf of all, like trustees, and the ordinary clansmen and women believed they had a blood relationship with the founder of their clan.

There were two way duties and obligations. An inadequate chief could be deposed and replaced by someone of greater ability.

Clan people had an immense pride in race. Their relationship with the chief was like adult children to a father and they had a real dignity.

The concept of clanship is very old and a more feudal notion of authority gradually crept in.

Pictland, for instance, was divided into seven principalities ruled by feudal leaders who were the strongest and most charismatic leaders of their particular groups.

By the sixth century the 'British' kingdoms of Strathclyde, Lothian and Celtic Dalriada (Argyll) had emerged and Scotland, as one nation, began to take shape in the time of King Kenneth MacAlpin.

Some chiefs claimed descent from ancient kings which may not have been accurate in every case.

By the twelfth and thirteenth centuries the clans and families were more strongly brought under the central control of Scottish monarchs.

Lands were awarded and administered more and more under royal favour, yet the power of the area clan chiefs was still very great.

The long wars to ensure Scotland's

*"The spirit of the clan means much
to thousands of people"*

independence against the expansionist ideas of English monarchs extended the influence of some clans and reduced the lands of others.

Those who supported Scotland's greatest king, Robert the Bruce, were awarded the territories of the families who had opposed his claim to the Scottish throne.

In the Scottish Borders country – the notorious Debatable Lands – the great families built up a ferocious reputation for providing warlike men accustomed to raiding into England and occasionally fighting one another.

Chiefs had the power to dispense justice and to confiscate lands and clan warfare produced a society where martial virtues – courage, hardiness, tenacity – were greatly admired.

Gradually the relationship between the clans and the Crown became strained as Scottish monarchs became more orientated to life in the Lowlands and, on occasion, towards England.

The Highland clans spoke a different language, Gaelic, whereas the language of Lowland Scotland and the court was Scots and in more modern times, English.

Highlanders dressed differently, had different

customs, and their wild mountain land sometimes seemed almost foreign to people living in the Lowlands.

It must be emphasised that Gaelic culture was very rich and story-telling, poetry, piping, the clarsach (harp) and other music all flourished and were greatly respected.

Highland culture was different from other parts of Scotland but it was not inferior or less sophisticated.

Central Government, whether in London or Edinburgh, sometimes saw the Gaelic clans as a challenge to their authority and some sent expeditions into the Highlands and west to crush the power of the Lords of the Isles.

Nevertheless, when the eighteenth century Jacobite Risings came along the cause of the Stuarts was mainly supported by Highland clans.

The word Jacobite comes from the Latin for James – Jacobus. The Jacobites wanted to restore the exiled Stuarts to the throne of Britain.

The monarchies of Scotland and England became one in 1603 when King James VI of Scotland (1st of England) gained the English throne after Queen Elizabeth died.

A map of the clans' homelands

The Union of Parliaments of Scotland and England, the Treaty of Union, took place in 1707.

Some Highland clans, of course, and Lowland families opposed the Jacobites and supported the incoming Hanoverians.

After the Jacobite cause finally went down at Culloden in 1746 a kind of ethnic cleansing took place. The power of the chiefs was curtailed. Tartan and the pipes were banned in law.

Many emigrated, some because they wanted to, some because they were evicted by force. In addition, many Highlanders left for the cities of the south to seek work.

Many of the clan lands became home to sheep and deer shooting estates.

But the warlike traditions of the clans and the great Lowland and Border families lived on, with their descendants fighting bravely for freedom in two world wars.

Remember the men from whence you came, says the Gaelic proverb, and to that could be added the role of many heroic women.

The spirit of the clan, of having roots, whether Highland or Lowland, means much to thousands of people.

Chapter two:

Clever and cunning

Great tracts of Upper Deeside are still owned by the Farquharson family.

The remarkable rise of the Farquharsons, who have dominated the area for over 500 years, stems from one Alexander "ciar", meaning dark or dusky, who was descended from the ancient lineage of the Thanes of Fife. The rapid rise of the family from this one incomer in the early 14th century was due to organised marriages. A judicious choice of bride meant that the family lands spread out from the Braes of Mar, through Invercauld and Aberarder via marriage to Isabel, only daughter and heiress of a Duncan Stewart. Their son, Findlay or "Findla mor" (Great Findlay) was the first Farquharson of Invercauld and the first of this remarkable family to play a fighting role in Scottish history. He was the Royal Standard bearer at the Battle of Pinkie where he met his death in 1547, his political involvement with the highest in the land setting a precedent for his many descendants.

Their ability not only to marry well, but to

further enhance their fortunes were also a strong family characteristic.

About 1541, one Donald Farquharson was made ballie of Strathdee. At this time he succeeded his half-brother to the families' lands. All told he fathered 10 sons and three daughters.

The second son, Robert 'departed from his father's halls' following some disagreement in the family. Turning round three times, 'as was proper and decorous of a man of his position with eyes closed, he tossed his stick into the air, and following the direction indicated by its fall arrived at Dundee, where he became a carpenter'.

Some time later a senior scion of the Mackintosh clan (a family with which the Farquharsons were much entwined) arrived with Margaret, his daughter, a young widow, who had been married to a Glengarry. They were on a visit to some relatives. Robert passed daily under the window curious as to his identity.

Margaret began to fall in love with this handsome young figure passing her window and, according to the story, not knowing how to further her acquaintance, began to pine away.

Mackintosh decided to cure her himself, after

none of the Dundee doctors could diagnose her ailment. Finally, she burst into tears and admitted to her father the reason for her misery.

Accordingly, the following morning Robert was halted in the street by a tall and fine old Highlander who informed him of the havoc he was causing. This did not impress the carpenter, but the old warrior was undaunted, 'stop until you see Maggy, and then you can give herself the denial,' he suggested.

As the daughter tripped in, Mackintosh made use of his military strategy and slipped out. Exactly what happened is unknown but like all the best romances and fairy stories, the result was clear because soon after this Robert and Margaret were married.

Margaret not only brought with her a handsome dowry, but astute sense of financial wheedling. Despite his initial scepticism, Robert was to find he had married well.

Returning with his bride to Deeside, Robert set up as a miller first at Crathie but due to the sparse amount of cultivated land in his local area, he upped and moved to a more prosperous site at Birse, fifteen miles away.

The local laird of the Finzean estate at Birse was a fast spender and sought loans from all his tenants. Mrs. Farquharson spotted this weakness and cunningly sent Robert on rent day, suggesting that he made sure the laird could catch sight of Robert's over-flowing purse. The ruse was successful and sure enough, it was not long before the laird applied to them for a loan. The miller granted the loan on the security of the mill and the adjoining farm. No sooner had the laird spent the loan than he returned to ask for another. Robert, meanwhile, was beginning to doubt the wisdom of such a policy, until his wife pointed out the long-term advantages of such leniency. This mortgaging system continued until the laird coincided with Mrs. Farquharson having no more money left to lend to him – in fact she was just at that moment going to the castle to ask for her loans back.

The laird had nothing left to offer but his estates. Robert and Margaret accepted this offer, and the Farquharson family spread their ownership of lands even further eastwards.

Chapter three:

Execution and deportation

Of the many colourful Farquharsons who took up arms on behalf of the Jacobite cause, few escaped lightly.

Typical of these supporters of Bonnie Prince Charlie was John Farquharson of Allargue (on Strathdon) who was 33 years in 1745. He left his wife and six young children to fight for the cause but was captured at the Battle of Culloden. Transported to London and kept for several years on a hulk of a Government vessel in appalling conditions, worse was in store. He was sentenced to death, along with two more young Highlanders. However, on the morning of his execution, he was reprieved, but ordered to be deported.

John Farquharson's cousin Francis of Monaltrie (or Monaltry) was also captured at Culloden and exiled.

About 1760, an old woman found that bathing in a spring at Pannaich, some two miles away

on the bank of the Dee, was good for her skin disease. Col. Francis, on return from exile decided to exploit the old woman's discovery. In 1770, in addition to building a lodge at the spring itself (now the Pannanich Wells Hotel), he set about developing the present site of Ballater, adjacent to his own seat at Monaltrie House.

In 1795, the Rev. Charles McHardy, referred to the late Mr. Farquharson of Monaltry as "That gentleman, with laudable spirit of patriotism, was the first person who undertook (and) made roads in Aberdeenshire, which he carried out with considerable exertion, and at great expense, for several years before 1745. On obtaining his liberty he immediately resumed his public-spirited improvements, chiefly in the five parishes of Ballater, Crathie, Glenmuick, Tullich and Glengarden. He was ably supported by Mr. Farquharson of Invercauld."

He died in 1790, but the work was completed by his son William Farquharson (1753-1828), to whom the monument on a low hill near Tullich was erected in 1830.

The Farquharsons, fathers and son, chose well, for the combination of the River Dee, the woods to the south, and the rocky hump of Craigendarroch to the North make Ballater a most attractive holiday centre.

Chapter four:

Colonel Anne

**Anne Farquharson daughter of the 9th Laird
became the wife of Aeneas Mackintosh, 22nd Laird
of Mackintosh of Moy, by Inverness. On the face
of it this was another splendid match for the
Farquharson family. Anne was also, like her
forebears, a highly political character.**

Lady Anne had long cherished hopes of
winning her husband over to the Prince's cause. She
was passionately attached to him, but when she learnt
that he had entered into definite engagements with
Lord President Forbes, she refused to see him again. In
a splendid act of defiance, she raised 600 men, half of
whom were sent to join the Prince, before the battle of
Falkirk, the other half she kept to protect Moy against
her husband and Lord Loudoun.

Bonnie Prince Charlie was received by Anne
on the 16th February, 1746, and shortly around that
time, Anne had cunningly managed to deceive an
attempt by 1500 Government troops to capture Moy.
Five of her retainers had effected a ruse by which
they had convinced the government leaders that an

entire Jacobite army was billeted within and close to Moy. The troops fled, and Lady Anne was nicknamed 'Colonel Anne' for what became known as the 'Rout of Moy.'

Her husband, in the meantime was taken prisoner by the Jacobites at Dornoch.

The Prince had the happy idea of sending him into the custody of 'Colonel Anne.'

It is said that when he was presented to her by his guards, she greeted him with a brief "your servant, Colonel." Legend has it that they addressed each other by these titles all their remaining lives.

Lady Anne was captured after Culloden, but set free after six weeks confinement in Inverness. She died in 1757.

Chapter five:

The Black Colonel

The chief of the Farquharson clan's home, Braemar Castle, had been built for the Earl of Mar in 1628, following the return of the estranged estates of the Earldom to the Erskine family by Mary Queen of Scots in 1565. But the castle had been fired and destroyed by its then owner, one of the most colourful of the Farquharsons, John, and the "Black Colonel".

The Black Colonel put his home to the torch to foil an attempt by the Government troops, sent in search of Bonnie Dundee and the Jacobites after the rising in 1689. The Black Colonel realised that Braemar Castle was to be used as a garrison base for the government forces and put paid to any plans of the commander by destroying it before their very eyes.

By a stroke of irony and good fortune, almost a century later, this very castle was subsequently totally renovated as a Hanoverian garrison in 1748, and was eventually returned, conveniently restored and rebuilt by the loathed redcoats, to the original Farquharsons after the garrison left in 1797.

The Black Colonel had appeared in many stories of the time, but his first brush with authority was many years earlier.

A local sheriff, John Gordon of Braikley, had apparently imposed fines on many who had been caught poaching fish, cattle rustling or generally throwing their weight around. Most of the culprits had paid up their fines, or agreed to settle in a friendly fashion – probably by some reciprocal agreement with the sheriff. But Braikley refused to settle in such a friendly fashion with the Black Colonel.

The Black Colonel was on his way to the market, fully armed, and sent John Ferguson, minister of Glenmuick, to settle their fines on the same terms as their neighbours. But for reasons, which have never been clearly understood, Braikley was having none of it, and gathered his friends and attacked the Black Colonel and his band.

Having 'loused' several shotts', against the Black Colonel, their fire was returned and in the ensuing skirmish, Braikley, his brother William and their cousin were killed and on the other side three met their deaths. It might have been very much a neighbourhood dispute, but because the Black Colonel was involved in the killing of a local man of the law, the matter was soon in the hands of the highest in the land.

On 12th February 1685, the Earl of Perth, Lord Chancellor, issued a warrant for apprehending John Farquharson of Inverey, alias the "Black Colonel" and other of his followers, who had been 'outlawed for the murder of the Baron of Braikley, in Glenmuick in 1666.'

The defence set forth by The Black Colonel friends was that he was captain of the watch at the time and had been following the custom, which was to go to the market with a like number of men to guard it.

"It is very weel known that the custome of the countery is that people who are going to the mercat – go allonst with companie, either for their own securitie of kindness, – moreover it is the custome to go with arms."

But the arrest was never made, as the Black Colonel escaped and hid as an outlaw in the many hills of the area. However, his pursuers never gave up the chase, and ten years later, when many of his escapades had already gone into local folklore, he was entertaining his old friend, the laird of Daldownie, at his castle at Inverey.

The story went that "after dinner", which was

strong and solid, it pleased them to be jolly, so they set about it accordingly, which appeared to include drinking many of the bottles on the table.

By chance, further down the glen at Aboyne, an old beggar woman was positioned outside the alehouse, begging. At some point a squadron of dragoons rode up.

"Giving her best curtesy to the officers, and her second best curtsey to the privates, while secretly wishing them to be in a country as red as their coats and very hot indeed, (i.e. in the flames of hell) she duly received a few coins." Hanging about the rear of the group, the beggar overheard the purpose of their errand up from Aberdeen. They were in pursuit of the Black Colonel.

"Realising the value of this news, she silently slipped away and stashing her wallet, hose and shoes under a bush for security she set forth for Inverey. The officers, prudently, decided to rest at Aboyne till darkness to avoid rousing suspicions, giving the old woman a good headstart up the road."

She then set off on what was a substantial trek through the glen of the Dee, an ambitious walk for anyone, and especially a woman of advanced years. The story recounts that:

"This route however, over Dinnet moor, through the pass of Ballater past the mouth of the Gairn and on up the Dee towards Crathie, before crossing the treacherous river some thirty miles above Aboyne was not for the faint hearted. Puffing away, the beggar sped on spurred by the weight of the information she carried, and no doubt the prospect of the reward on offer."

Meanwhile up at the castle, the colonel and the laird of Daldownie had recently retired, "a little top-heavy, to their beds". Just as the troopers forded the river the beggar awoke the slumbering colonel. Rushing naked down the stairs, the colonel and Daldownie fled the stronghold in the direction of the Ey. "Each of their strides covered 18 feet" and they soon reached the river. The Ey was in spate that night and a raging torrent, but the Black Colonel cleared it with one alimighty leap giving the bridge of that place today its name, "Drochaid-an-Leum" (the bridge of the leap). The colonel and Daldownie forded through the stream where a horse would have been swept away, and the pair stood thus as the troopers drew up to the castle.

With a furious rush, for there had been a large reward on the colonel's head for some time, the soldiers smashed on the castle door. With one bang it swung open. In their haste the pair had left it unlocked. After a fruitless search of the building, which produced no fugitives, the officer ordered the place to be fired. Standing guard at the door to apprehend the colonel should he have hidden, a tall figure burst out and was immediately arrested. "Yield or die," roared the guard, to which the reply was "Gabh an Donas thu," (the devil take you,) and a hale whack on the guard's sconce, (head) who was sent tumbling down the doorsteps. The light of the burning castle was strong enough to show that the detainee was Annie Ban, the colonel's mistress, who descended the stairs and stepped lightly over the prone guard. Although the redcoats realised they had lost their quarry, they let Annie pass, perhaps ignorant of the fact that she was carrying clothes belonging to the Black Colonel.

In the meantime, upon Creagan Chait, the hill above the castle, the colonel and Daldownie watched as the redcoats attempted to set light to the castle.

Suddenly the colonel burst out "laughing and dancing fit to better a madman."

Daldownie, shocked by this outburst, tried to calm him, but the colonel was beside himself with mirth. While the tears rolled down the colonel's face, he explained that the charter-room had recently been filled with powder, and he hoped that they would soon see the redcoats being blown up as well as the castle. But sadly for the Colonel, the flames leapt right up into the fire, and although the interior of the castle was destroyed, the walls still stood, and so did the surrounding soldiers, quite unharmed.

Seeing this, the still naked Black Colonel apparently stormed and foamed, stamping at the ground in a fearful frenzy.

The Colonel, now homeless and endlessly chased by the soldiers, took refuge in a cave just up the river, under an overhanging slab of rock, still known to this day as the colonel's bed, where he was brought food and clothing by the doughty Annie. For such an eventful life, the Colonel died peacefully in old age, and safely in bed. Having made clear that he wished to be buried in the graveyard near his home amid the area of his many exploits at the Chapel of the Maidens at Inverey, somehow this request was overlooked by those responsible for the interring. By mistake, apparently he was ceremonially laid to rest in Braemar. But in death, as in life, the Colonel was one for surprises.

The next day, the coffin appeared to have

moved in the night, and was now sticking above ground. It was rapidly re-buried, only to find that this mysterious rising occurred over three successive nights.

Finally, the colonel's old retainers, remembering his request, piled the coffin on a raft and brought it up the River Ey from Braemar to the graveyard beside his old castle at Inverey, and he rested until many years later.

A couple of workmen were digging down for another burial when they accidentally prodded the crumbling coffin of the old colonel. Realising that this was the Black Colonel himself, they decided to take a tooth each as a memento.

They were soon to regret their action. That night both claimed to have been visited by the ghost of a furious Black Colonel, demanding the return of his molars. The gravediggers wasted no time in complying with his wish, and tossed them back into the grave as soon as dawn broke.

Chapter six:

A family cursed

The 'modern' House of Invercauld is a splendid edifice East of Braemar on Deeside. It was from this castle, described as the Castleton of Mar, where the Farquharsons had left to fight and spread their might over their harassed neighbours. Later generations entertained Queen Victoria to the Annual Gathering.

That the family still occupy the estate to this day is the most remarkable fact about Invercauld, considering the curse with which it was inflicted.

The origins of this curse appear to be rooted in fact, if not accurately in time.

In the skirmishes between the occupiers of the lands of the North East in the fifteenth or perhaps sixteenth centuries a Lamont of Inverey was hanged on a pine tree. The pine tree stood on a knoll just to the west of Mar Lodge Bridge.

The bare bones of the story go thus.

A man called Lamont, who lived at Inverey, the hamlet that lies west of Braemar and site of the now vanished Inverey Castle of Black Colonel fame, had assisted a rival clan in one of their battles. When the enemy clan were beating a retreat they left Lamont to the mercy of his close neighbours, with whom he had previously fallen out.

The Farquharsons 'planted' some sheep in one of Lamont's limekilns, which were then 'found' and therefore rendered Lamont guilty of sheep stealing. This was a very convenient crime, as hanging was the traditional remedy.

Lamont must of course have been unwilling to be dragged to the stout pine tree and when the hangman's rope was tightened Lamont's widowed mother cursed the Farquharsons or Clan Fhionnlaidh.

"This tree will flourish high and broad,
Green as it grows today,
When from the banks o' the bonnie Dee,
Clan Fhionnlaidh's all away".

At the time, the Farquharsons owned huge areas of the Dee valley, and appeared invincible, and their fighting spirit carried them along for some time. But it was not to last.

You can judge for yourself if you look in the Invercauld Aisle in the Braemar Churchyard at but one small section of the family.

"Sacred to the memory of John Farquharson

of Invercauld, who died in 1750. Sacred also to the memory of James Farquharson of Invercauld his son who died in 24th June 1805; and Amelia, Lady Sinclair, his spouse (daughter of Lord James Murray) who died in 1779. They had eleven children, all of whom with the exception of the youngest, Catherine, died before them. Mary, Matilda, Jane, John and George lie interred with their parents in the ground joining; Charlotte in Arnhall; Fanny at Lisbon; and Amelia, Margaret and Ann in the burying ground in North Leith."

To this day, the inheritor of the Farquharsons of Invercauld has not passed by direct descent.